Pebble® Plus

Aircraft

Jet Planes

by Mari Schuh

Consulting Editor: Gail Saunders-Smith, PhD

Consultant: Stewart W. Bailey, Curator
Evergreen Aviation & Space Museum
McMinnville, Oregon

CAPSTONE PRESS
a capstone imprint

Pebble Plus is published by Capstone Press,
1710 Roe Crest Drive, North Mankato, Minnesota 56003
www.capstonepub.com

Library of Congress Cataloging-in-Publication Data
Cataloging-in-publication information is on file with the Library of Congress.
978-1-62065-113-1 (library binding)
978-1-4765-1070-5 (eBook PDF)

Editorial Credits
Erika L. Shores, editor; Heidi Thompson, designer; Eric Manske, production specialist

Photo Credits
Newscom: A3582 Alexander Ruesche Deutsch Presse Agentur, 13, ZUMA Press, 17;
Shutterstock: Carlos E. Santa Maria, 11, Ilja Masik, cover, 21, Josef Hanus, 9, Lukich, 19, MC_PP, 5, Timurpix, 15, tr3gin, 7

Artistic Effects
Shutterstock: New Line

The author dedicates this book to Sam Krizek of Racine, Wisconsin.

Note to Parents and Teachers

The Aircraft set supports national science standards related to science, technology, and society.
This book describes and illustrates jet planes. The images support early readers in understanding
the text. The repetition of words and phrases helps early readers learn new words. This book also
introduces early readers to subject-specific vocabulary words, which are defined in the Glossary
section. Early readers may need assistance to read some words and to use the Table of Contents,
Glossary, Read More, Internet Sites, and Index sections of the book.

Printed in the United States of America.
032018   000289

Table of Contents

Jet Planes

Listen to the engines roar!

A jet plane takes off

from the runway.

Whoosh! Jets are 10 times

faster than cars.

Parts of Jet Planes

Jet planes have powerful engines.

Jet engines shoot out

streams of hot gas that push

the plane forward.

Two long wings lift jet planes
high into the sky.
The wings also hold fuel tanks.

Pilots fly jets from the cockpit.
Cockpit instruments show
how fast and how high
the jet is flying.

Kinds of Jets

Airliners are big jets filled with seats for many passengers. These jets fly more than 500 miles (805 kilometers) per hour.

Business jets are smaller than airliners. Business jets have roomy seats, couches, and kitchens. Companies and governments use these jets.

Cargo jets are big airplanes without seats.

These jets deliver everything from mail to helicopters.

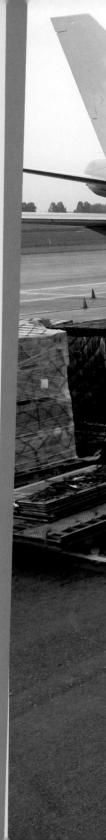

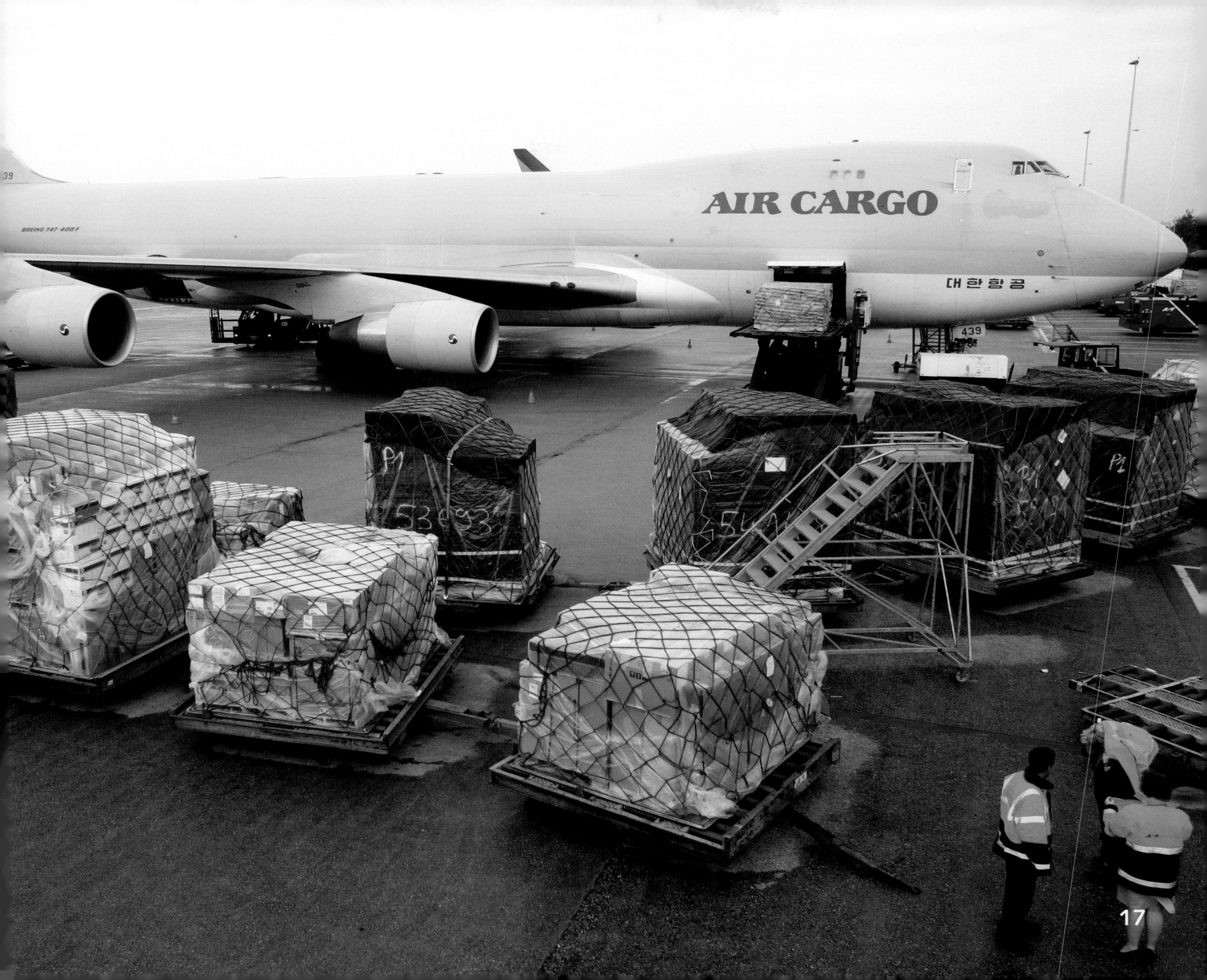
BOEING 747-400F
AIR CARGO
대한항공
439

Fighter jets fight battles
in the air.
These fast jets can
quickly change direction.

Up, Up, and Away!

Look up! A jet streaks across
the sky. Jets fly nearly 7 miles
(11 kilometers) above you.

Why Are
We Getting
a Divorce?

Other books by
Peter Mayle and Arthur Robins
available from Harmony Books

Baby Taming
Sweet Dreams and Monsters

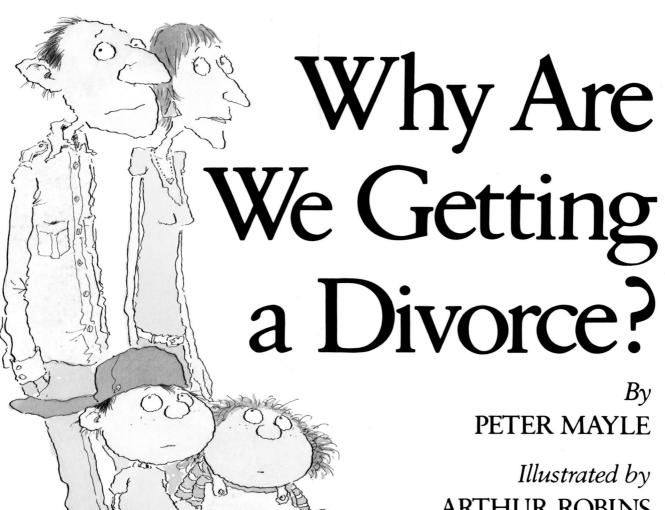

Why Are We Getting a Divorce?

By

PETER MAYLE

Illustrated by

ARTHUR ROBINS

HARMONY BOOKS / NEW YORK

This book was previously published in a different form as *Divorce Can Happen to the Nicest People*.

Published by Harmony Books, a division of Crown Publishers, Inc., 201 East 50th Street, New York, New York 10022. Member of the Crown Publishing Group.

Random House, Inc. New York, Toronto, London, Sydney, Auckland

HARMONY and colophon are trademarks of Crown Publishers, Inc.

Book design by Clair Moritz

Manufactured in China

Library of Congress Cataloging-in-Publication Data

Mayle, Peter.
Why Are We Getting a Divorce?
Summary: A handbook offering "reassurance, sympathy, and sound advice on how to cope with a family that is splitting up."
1. Divorce—Juvenile literature   [1. Divorce]
I. Robins, Arthur, ill.   II. Title.
HQ814.M34   1988   306.8′9   87-12105

ISBN 0-517-56527-7

10   9   8   7   6   5   4   3

DIVORCE CAN HAPPEN TO THE NICEST PEOPLE

Do you know how many people separate and get divorced every year?

Millions and millions and millions.

Old people, young people, rich people, poor people, black people, white people, people all the way from Alaska to Australia.

More people get divorced in a single day than you could squeeze into a giant football stadium.

More people get divorced in a single year than the entire population of New York.

And yet, strangely enough when you think how many times it happens, divorce is often treated like some rare and awful disease. Something to be whispered about. Something to be ashamed of. As though there was something wrong with people who get divorced.

Of course, that's nonsense. Nothing that happens millions of times a year can be called unusual or rare. And all those millions of people can't be bad, just because they get divorced.

In fact, most of them are nice men and women. Like your mother and father, for instance.

1

Divorce is very sad, but it's a fact of life. And the first thing you should try to understand is that you're not a freak if it happens in your family. Your parents aren't monsters. You aren't unusual. (If there was ever a school for the kids of divorced or separated parents, it would have to be the biggest school in the world!) You're just unlucky.

You know how you're always being told that you should do this or you should do that? Well, it's different when you're trying to understand divorce. It's the shouldn'ts that are important. And these three are probably the most important:

You shouldn't make the mistake of thinking that your parents don't love you anymore because they're getting divorced.

You shouldn't think that the whole thing is somehow your fault, because it *never* is.

And you shouldn't put the blame on one parent, because divorce is never only one person's fault.

Like anything else in life, divorce is easier to cope with if you have some idea of why it happens. And that's what we're going to try to explain. So let's start at the beginning, because you can't have a divorce unless you have had a marriage first.

3

WHY YOUR PARENTS GOT MARRIED

With all those millions of divorces every year, you may wonder why people get married in the first place. Let's take your mother and father as an example and see what happened with them.

A long time ago, before you were born, they met and liked each other. And the more they saw of each other, the more they wanted to be together. One date a week turned into three or four dates a week. And after a while, they were seeing each other every day.

This next part may be hard for you to believe now, but your mother and father fell in love. They wanted to be together all the time. They wanted to share a bed. They wanted to share a home. They wanted to share a whole life. They hated the idea of being apart.

When you feel like that, living in separate houses is no fun at all. So your mother and father decided to live together.

So why didn't they leave it at that? After all, there are plenty of men and women who live together without being married. Why couldn't your parents have done the same?

If you had been able to ask them that question at the time, they would probably have told you that they wanted to have children. That they wanted to be one family instead of two separate people. And in our society, the way to make that official is to get married.

Marriage tells everybody in the world what the man and the woman have been telling each other. It takes their private promise and turns it into a public, legal agreement. And it's been going on for a long, long time.

Nobody knows for sure when the first ever marriage took place, but we do know that the ancient Greeks were getting married as far back as three thousand years ago. The fact that people are still getting married today proves that it's a tradition that most men and women like. It shows that the man and the woman are prepared to do their best to stay together, and raise their children together. As we said, they don't *always* get married, but most people do. It's one of the many differences between human beings and other living things.

Some birds, for instance, don't have much of a family life. Often, the father bird may not even see his own babies; the mother is left to raise them on her own. And after quite a short time—just a few weeks—even the mother's had enough. The young ones are given a friendly shove and have to go and take care of themselves.

That's the way it is with dogs, cats and most other animals. The idea of a family as we know it hardly exists.

We humans are different. First, because it's usual for both parents to help raise their children. And second, because the children don't leave home until they are young adults. They might have had as much as twenty years of living with their parents before going out into the world on their own.

As you're finding out, it doesn't always work that way. But don't ever think that your parents got married with the idea of getting divorced later. It wouldn't make sense. Everyone who gets married hopes and truly believes that it will last forever.

Your parents have decided to live apart. Even though they thought they never would. Even though they tried to stay happily married. Even though they still love you.

And if you think that sounds crazy, wait until you read some of the reasons people give for getting divorced.

WHAT GOES WRONG?

There are two sizes of reasons why people get divorced. The big reason, which we will come to in a minute, and a whole lot of smaller reasons, some serious and some silly. Here are just a few:

"He's so grouchy in the mornings he's like a bear with a sore head."

"She smokes in bed."

"He never notices what I wear."

"She always leaves the top off the toothpaste."

"He eats too much."

"She's always on a diet."

"He snores."

"*She* snores."

And so on. They're more like complaints, really. And when you think about them, they don't seem very important. But they become bigger, more important and more annoying when two people aren't happy living with each other. What you find sweet and funny when you love someone can drive you crazy when you don't.

11

And that's the real reason for divorce: not enough love. Just as two people can fall in love, they can fall out of love, too. If that happens, like it has with your parents, it's very, very hard for two people to go on living together.

Nobody has ever been able to say exactly what makes one person fall in love with another. It's a complicated mixture of feelings, needs and likes and dislikes that is totally different from person to person.

What makes people fall *out* of love, though, is a little easier to understand. It's because they change.

Think back a couple of years. Can you remember what games you liked playing best? Or the friends you liked to be with? Do you still like to play the same games? Do you still have the same friends? The chances are that without really noticing it, you're different now from the way you were then. You've changed.

Adults are supposed to have gotten through most of their changing by the time they get married. They're supposed to know what they want and how they want to live. And for a time, most married couples want the same things. (Your mother and your father both wanted you, for instance.)

But the truth is that people don't remain the same, no matter how old they are. All of us change throughout our lives. And that's where the problems can start.

Everyone changes in different ways and at different times. Some married people can adjust to the changes that are going on. But sometimes they come along so suddenly or seem so big that it's like living with someone you hardly know. Two people who used to be in love have turned into strangers.

When that happens, it makes living together more and more difficult. Both people become unhappy. Those silly little habits like leaving the top off the toothpaste tube or falling asleep in front of the TV gradually become more annoying. So instead of laughter, couples have arguments, and look for excuses to be apart. They spend less and less time together. Then one day, they have to admit that even with all the trying in the world, the marriage just won't work.

If there are no children involved, it's easier to agree that the marriage was a sad mistake, and the best thing is for both of them to go their separate ways.

13

But when there are children, it's so much harder. Should parents stay together and pretend to be happy, and hope that the kids won't notice that they're not? Or should they split up, so each one has the chance to be happy with someone else?

Your mother and father have decided to split up. They thought about it and worried about how it would affect you before they decided to get a divorce. But their hope is that they—and you—will all be happier in the long run because of what they've done. It's hard for you to believe that now, but wait and see. They could just be right.

OTHER MEN AND WOMEN

As if there weren't already plenty of reasons why people get divorced, here's one more. And it's important enough to tell you about separately.

It often happens when two people are changing and having their troubles. Right out of the blue, without any warning, one of them meets someone else and falls in love.

More problems, more complications, more unhappiness. It's sad and difficult for everyone.

If you're the parent who has fallen in love with someone else, it's one of the hardest things in the world to tell your children.

If you're the other parent, you feel more lonely and miserable than ever.

If you're one of the children, it's confusing and upsetting to have to accept a "new" parent.

And if you're the someone else, it's hard because you feel you're making extra problems for everyone.

Nobody plans it, but that's the way it often is. We'd like to be able to say that there's a quick and simple cure for all this unhappiness and confusion, but there isn't. The only cure that works is time.

LIVING WITH HALF YOUR PARENTS

In time, you'll find that living with one more-or-less happy parent is better than living with two unhappy parents. But nobody will say that the first few months of this new kind of life are easy.

No matter how much you might feel like you want to split yourself in two, you can't. You have to get used to living with one parent and visiting the other one. And in the beginning, there may not be a lot of visits. Divorced people often get very angry with each other and need time apart to sort out their feelings.

When parents divorce, it's usually (but not always) the father who moves out of the house. And until you understand why, you're bound to think he doesn't love you as much as your mother does. How could he? He walked out and left you. But there are a couple of good reasons why your father goes and your mother stays.

First, the family home should be for the family. It would be very unfair if your father kept the home for himself and made the rest of you go and look for another place to live.

The second reason is that your mother, even if she works at a job outside of the home, is probably still a lot better at looking after you and your home than your father is. Mothers usually are. Your dad may be a great cook and a whizz at doing the ironing, but most fathers aren't.

You see? It's not a question of which parent loves you the most but which parent can take care of you the best. Once you realize

that, it might help you feel a little less sad about living with one parent and only visiting the other.

There's no magic way to cheer yourself up. Feeling sorry for yourself is only going to make you more miserable, which will make your mother and father more miserable. And if you feel that you're the only one having a bad time, think about the bad times your parents are going through as well.

Remember, your mother loves you very much. Remember, your father loves you very much. And remember, being unhappy doesn't last.

WHO'S RIGHT? WHO'S WRONG? WHO'S TO BLAME?

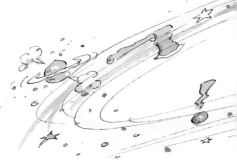

From the day you trip and blame your shoelaces to the day your false teeth fall in the soup and you blame your dentist, you're always looking for someone to blame when life goes wrong. We all do. It's human nature. If you're upset, it *has* to be someone else's fault.

Divorce is one of the biggest upsets there is in life. Everybody involved wants to blame somebody else. And who do you see when you look around for somewhere to place the blame? Your parents. You may feel that they have done all this on purpose just to make you sad and angry. You know it's not your fault, so it must be theirs. And of course, it is. But the trouble is that it's not easy to be fair when you're upset.

If you could divide the blame equally between parents, perhaps that would make some sense, but you never can. You might put most of the blame on your father because he's gone away and left you. You might blame your mother because she's in love with someone other than your father. Almost always, though, kids like yourself take sides with one parent while the other one is left standing alone. Sad to say, parents themselves often encourage this. They're upset too, and they're looking for someone to blame. And they usually blame each other.

18

It's difficult for you to be fair when neither of them is being fair. Divorced parents are often not only nasty *to* each other. They're nasty *about* each other. And you sometimes get caught in the middle of it all. It makes you feel as if you are watching a boxing match, with words being used instead of fists.

There isn't much to be cheerful about while this is going on. All we can say is that people can't stay mad at each other forever. They calm down, and they realize that there are better things to do than spend their time and energy being angry with someone. That goes for you too, so when you get mad, talk about your feelings with someone like your mother, your father, your best friend—anyone you feel comfortable with. Don't get involved in your parents' arguments. Two people fighting in one family is quite enough without you joining in.

And try as hard as you can not to take sides, because divorce is never just one parent's fault.

19

AT LAST THE GOOD NEWS

Divorce isn't all bad. There is a bright side, as long as you and your parents are prepared to give it a chance.

Let's say you're living with your mother and you visit your father on weekends or during vacations. Even though you've known him all your life, those first visits are bound to feel strange. It's strange to see him living in a different place, maybe with somebody else, and it's strange to have to say good-bye at the end of your visit.

After a while, though, you get used to the idea that divorce doesn't mean good-bye forever. And then, little by little, visit by visit, you'll begin to find that maybe life isn't so sad and bad after all. There are even a couple of advantages you get only when your parents are divorced. We're not saying that they make up for not living with both parents, but they help. For instance:

Making friends with two new people

When you spend time with your mother and father separately, something interesting happens. You start to see each of them as individual people rather than parents; they start to see you as a person as well as their child.

Because they aren't busy with each other, they can spend a little more time talking to you, listening to you and getting to know you. This feels funny, but good. It's like finding two new friends whom you know you're going to like for a long time.

21

AN EXTRA LIFE

When you lived with both of your parents, you had one kind of life. Now that you're living with or visiting each parent, but separately, you have the chance of trying two lives, and they'll be very different.

Your mother will have her friends. Your father will have his. You'll meet them all. Your mother will have her way of doing things. Your father will have his. You'll be able to try both.

Your father might like:

sunbathing on Christmas Eve
old movies on TV
pizza
breakfast in bed
small Siamese cats
football
Donald Duck

Your mother might like:

a white Christmas
going to the theater
hamburgers
walks in the rain
big hairy dogs
ice skating
Bruce Springsteen

We just made up that list, but you get the idea: when you share two separate lives with two separate people, it can be very interesting. Better still, it can be a lot of fun. And that's something you never thought you'd get when your parents divorced.

PARENTS NEED ALL THE HELP THEY CAN GET

One more time, think what getting divorced must be like for your mother and father.

It's a mess. They're sad, angry and upset. They're worried about you. And on top of that, everyday life is suddenly much harder to cope with. Each of them now has to do the chores that used to be shared between them.

Your mother not only has to take care of you and the house, as well as go to work, but she now finds herself with a whole new batch of problems. If the car breaks down, she has to get it fixed. If the garden is turning into a jungle, she has to clear it up. If the neighbors are having too many noisy parties, she has to go and complain. Problems that used to be shared with your father, she now has to solve on her own.

Meanwhile, your father isn't having too good a time either. In addition to working, and probably paying for two homes, he also has to do the chores around the house: cooking, cleaning, making the beds, shopping for food, organizing the laundry, and doing the dishes. He doesn't have anyone to share the work with either.

It's tough for both of them. But it can be a lot better if you make up your mind that you're going to help in every way you can.

First, you could try to forget how sad you are and remember how sad they are. Why don't you see if you can cheer them up instead of

waiting for them to cheer you up? (Telling your parents you love them is a pretty good start.)

Next, you could do your share of chores—or even a bit more than your share. Nobody's going to expect you to cook a seven-course dinner while you're doing the ironing, mowing the lawn and washing the car, but you can help out.

If you don't already help, tomorrow would be a great day to start doing things like making your own bed, tidying your own room, clearing away the dishes, washing out the tub after you have a bath and hanging up your clothes. These chores may be boring, but why should someone else have to do them?

The last way you can help is much more difficult, but it's also much more important.

For most mothers and fathers, the hardest part of divorce is worrying about the children. How will the children feel about their parents? Will they end up hating their mother, or their father or both of them? Will they be too upset to cope with school? The list of worries goes on and on.

Now it's a fact that worries are worse when you keep them to yourself. The minute you can tell someone about them, they're somehow not quite so bad. And that's where you come in.

It's not always easy for parents to talk about divorce. They sometimes need a little nudge from you. This nudge could be asking them straight out to talk to you about what went wrong, or it could be showing them that you're not going to let even a big problem like divorce get you down.

How you do it doesn't matter, as long as you let them know that you love them enough to want to help.

Your parents made a mistake and they've been unlucky, just like millions and millions of other parents. You've been unlucky too, just like millions of other kids. In time, though, those kids all get over it. So will you. And so will your parents.

You'll see.